A New True Book

POLICE

By Ray Broekel

This "true book" was prepared under the direction of Illa Podendorf, formerly with the Laboratory School, University of Chicago

CHILDRENS PRESS, CHICAGO

PHOTO CREDITS

Courtesy of Chicago Police Department—cover, 2, 7, 12, 14, 15, 17, 19, 20 (top), 25, 29, 31, 32, 34, 39, 41, 44, 45

California Highway Patrol: Audio Visual Department—4, 8, 9, 10 (2 photos), 13 (2 photos), 20 (bottom), 22

City of Anaheim—23, 24, 27, 37

Chicago Fire Department—28, 42

Cover—Police officers walking their beat

Library of Congress Cataloging in Publication Data

Broekel, Ray.
Police.

(A New true book)
For grades 1-3.
SUMMARY: An introduction to the activities of our helpful police.
1. Police—Juvenile literature. [1. Police]
I. Title.
HV7922.B76 363.2 81-7693
ISBN 0-516-01643-1 AACR2

8 9 10 R 99 98 97 96 95 94 93

TABLE OF CONTENTS

THE POLICE

The police keep things going well.

They help people.

The police see that laws are followed.

They catch people who have done wrong.

Who can join the police?

Both men and women can.

They should be strong.

They should be well.

And they must take a test.

And pass it, too.

A ROOKIE

A new police person is called a rookie.

The rookie goes to police school.

The rookie learns how to handle guns.

The rookie learns first aid.

Rookies learn all about police work.

They learn traffic rules. Town and city laws are learned, too.

The rookie learns how to become a good policeman or police woman.

UNIFORMS

Most police uniforms are blue.

But in some places, police wear green or tan uniforms.

NSL 095

Pinto
Squire
653 HGQ

Most police hats have badges on them.

All police wear badges on their uniforms.

Every badge has a number on it.

Some police don't wear uniforms.

They wear street clothes.

These police are detectives.

They help find answers to questions. This helps solve crimes.

Police search a car.
Some of the police are in uniform.
Some are not.

EQUIPMENT

What are some kinds of police equipment?

- Gun belt and gun
- Nightstick
- Whistle
- Handcuffs
- Two-way radio

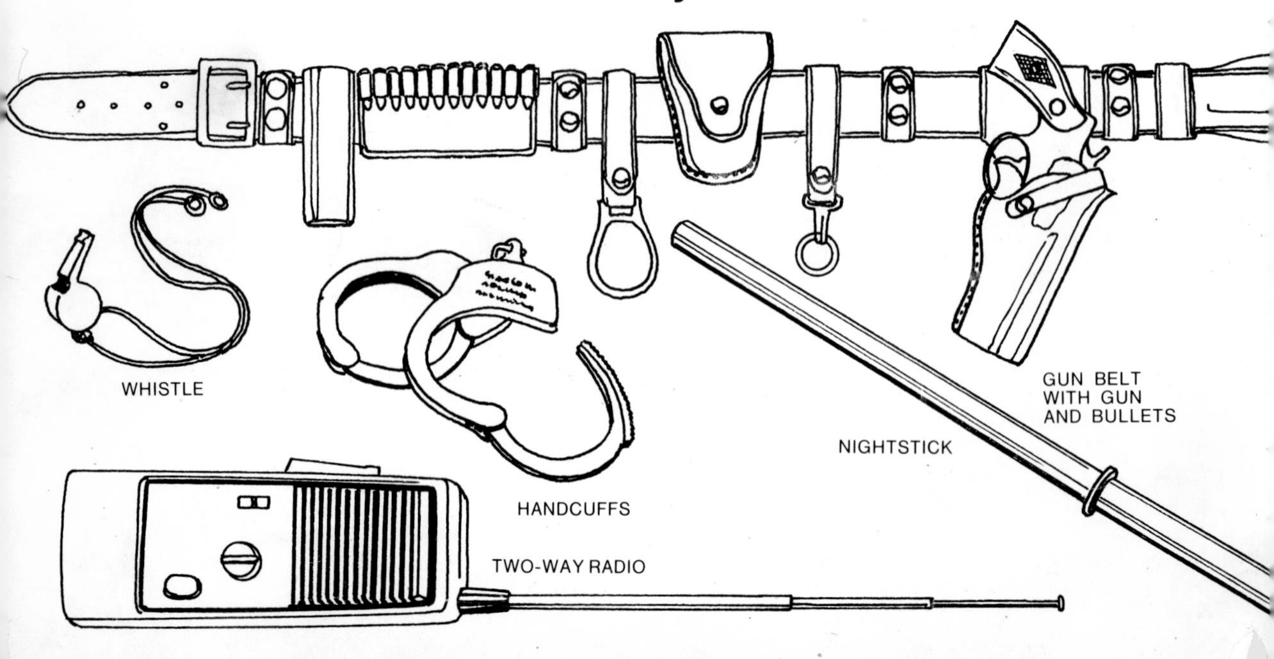

SOME POLICE DUTIES

Some police cover a "beat."

A beat is the part of a town or city a police person watches.

Some police walk their beats.

POLICE 9439
M 5462

HIGHWAY PATROL

Some ride in cars.

The cars sometimes use their flashing lights and sirens.

Some police ride motorcycles.

The cycles have two-way radios. With two-way radios police can talk to other police.

Police cars also have two-way radios.

And most police who walk their beats carry two-way radios.

Some cities have mounted police.

They find it easy to get around in traffic.

Police horses are well trained.

Helicopters are used by police in some big cities.

Police in helicopters watch over the cities by air.

Police also use helicopters to help them save people.

ANAHEIM
POLICE

Police boats are used in
some big cities, too.

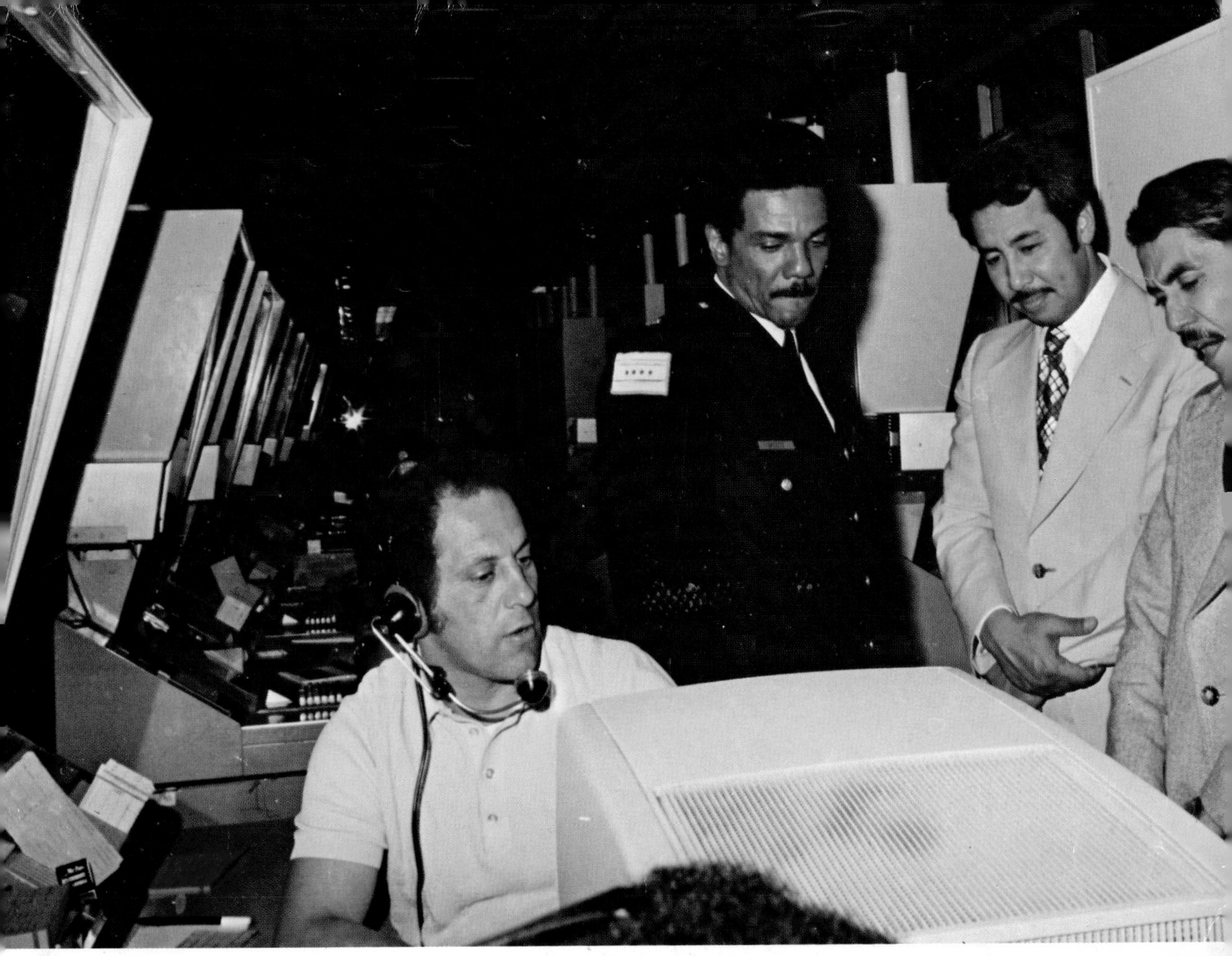

People often go to police stations to see how the police work.

An important police person is the dispatcher.

A dispatcher works in the police station.

One thing a dispatcher does is give out orders.

The two-way radio is used.

The dispatcher keeps in touch with all police working their beats.

Some police direct traffic.

They work at busy street corners.

Their job is to keep traffic moving.

The traffic police also help walkers cross streets safely.

SNOW ROUTE
NO PARKING
NO PARKING
BUS STOP
NO PARKING
POLISH
MEAT BA
Sandwich

Some police walk their beats.

They check stores and buildings.

They make sure things are going well.

They help people in trouble.

Some police are in patrol cars.

They ride around to make sure things are all right.

The dispatcher calls them if there is trouble somewhere else.

Then the patrol cars go there quickly.

Police know their town or city well.

They know where stores and buildings are.

The police know where different streets are.

They help people who are lost.

Some police work as safety officers.

They go into schools and give talks.

Safety rules are explained.

What do the officers talk about?

- Bicycle safety rules

- School bus safety rules

- Safety rules for walkers

Police look at fire damage. They want to see if the fire was an accident or not.

Police help fire fighters at a fire.

The police keep other people and traffic away from the fire.

That way the fire fighters can do their work.

Some towns have extra police.

They work only part time.

They may help with traffice during a parade.

Sometimes they help with the crowd at a big game.

Police have other helpers, too.

Crossing guards help police.

School safety patrols help.

The police help us in many ways.

That's why we should help them whenever we can.

WORDS YOU SHOULD KNOW

badge (BAJ)—something worn to show that a person belongs to a certain group

beat—a route or round that is followed regularly

crime (KRYM)—an action that is against the law

crowd (KROWD)—a large number of people gathered together

detective (de • TEK • tiv)—a police officer not in uniform whose work is solving crimes

different (DIF • er • ent)—not the same; unlike

direct (dih • REKT)—to guide; point

dispatcher (DIS • pach • er)—a person who sends messages quickly

explain (eks • PLAYN)—to make clear; to tell about

first aid—emergency care given to an injured or sick person

handcuffs (HAND • kufs)—pair of metal rings that can be put around the wrists of a prisoner

handle (HAN • dil)—to use or operate

helicopter (HEL • ih • kop • ter)—an aircraft without wings

law—a rule

motorcycle (MO • ter • sy • kil)—a vehicle with two wheels and a motor

mounted (MOUNT • id)—to get up on a horse

nightstick—a long piece of wood carried by police officers

officer (OFF • ih • ser)—a member of the police group

order—command

parade (pah • RAYD)— to pass before crowds of people with bands and vehicles

pass—to complete with good results

patrol (pah • TROLL)—to walk through an area to guard it

patrol car—a car which goes through an area to guard it

quick (KWIK)—fast, with speed

rookie (ROOK • ee)—a person with no experience; a beginner

safety officer (SAYF • tee OFF • ih • ser)—a person whose job it is to keep people from danger or harm

siren (SY • ren)—a device that makes a loud sound or noise

test—questions to find out a person's knowledge

traffic (TRAF • ik)—the movement of cars, trucks, and people along streets and roads

trouble (TRUB • uhl)—a problem; a different situation

uniform (YU • nih • form)—special clothes worn by members of a group

INDEX

About the Author

Ray Broekel is a full-time freelance writer who lives with his wife, Peg, and a dog, Fergus, in Ipswich, Massachusetts. He has had twenty years of experience as a children's book editor and newspaper supervisor, and has taught many subjects in kindergarten through college levels. Dr. Broekel has had over 1,000 stories and articles published, and over 100 books. His first book was published in 1956 by Childrens Press.